W9-ANU-098

Help Me Understand

Why Is Smoking Bad for Me?

Elizabeth Krajnik

PowerKiDS press™

NEW YORK

Published in 2019 by The Rosen Publishing Group, Inc.
29 East 21st Street, New York, NY 10010

First Edition

Editor: Elizabeth Krajnik
Book Design: Rachel Rising

Photo Credits: Cover, aslysun/Shutterstock.com; p. 4 gmstockstudio/Shutterstock.com; p. 5 Pe3k/Shutterstock.com; p. 7 aerogondo2/Shutterstock.com; p. 8 janews/Shutterstock.com; p. 9 Rocketclips, Inc./Shutterstock.com; p. 11 ArtFamily/Shutterstock.com; p. 12 risteski goce/Shutterstock.com; p. 13 karen roach/Shutterstock.com; p. 14 ChristianChan/Shutterstock.com; p. 15 IAN HOOTON/SPL/Science Photo Library/Getty Images; p. 17 Photographee.eu/Shutterstock.com; p. 18 LightField Studios/Shutterstock.com; p. 19 PhotoMediaGroup/Shutterstock.com; p. 21 Image Point Fr/Shutterstock.com; p. 22 Rob Marmion/Shutterstock.com; p. 22 (inset) petch one/Shutterstock.com.

Cataloging-in-Publication Data

Names: Krajnik, Elizabeth.
Title: Why is smoking bad for me? / Elizabeth Krajnik.
Description: New York : PowerKids Press, 2019. | Series: Help me understand | Includes glossary and index.
Identifiers: LCCN ISBN 9781508167327 (pbk.) | ISBN 9781508167303 (library bound) | ISBN 9781508167334 (6 pack)
Subjects: LCSH: Tobacco use–Prevention–Juvenile literature. | Youth–Tobacco use–Juvenile literature. | Smoking–Juvenile literature.
Classification: LCC HV5735.K73 2019 | DDC 362.29'6-dc23

Manufactured in the United States of America

CPSIA Compliance Information: Batch #CS18PK: For Further Information contact Rosen Publishing, New York, New York at 1-800-237-9932

Contents

What Are Cigarettes?............................ 4

Nicotine 6

Health Problems................................ 8

Changing How You Look........................ 10

Affecting Others 12

Peer Pressure 14

Why Do Adults Smoke?........................ 16

Breaking the Habit............................ 18

How to Quit 20

Why Is Smoking Bad? 22

Glossary 23

Index 24

Websites...................................... 24

What Are Cigarettes?

A cigarette is a small roll of paper filled with cut tobacco for smoking. Tobacco is a tall plant that produces leaves that are dried and chewed or used in cigarettes. Cigarettes have about 600 **ingredients** in them. When these ingredients are burned, they create more than 7,000 **chemicals**.

Some people smoke e-cigarettes. Instead of burning tobacco, e-cigarettes heat a liquid, or substance that flows freely like water, that becomes a vapor, or a substance in the form of a gas. The person breathes in the vapor just like people do cigarette smoke.

e-cigarettes

Of the 7,000 chemicals in cigarettes, at least 69 are known to cause **cancer**. Many other chemicals found in cigarettes are **poisonous**.

Nicotine

Nicotine is a chemical found in tobacco. It's very addicting, which means it causes addiction, or the state of being unable to give something up. That's why many people find it very hard to quit smoking. However, scientists don't believe nicotine causes cancer on its own.

When a person smokes a cigarette or e-cigarette, nicotine enters their bloodstream and makes them feel a rush of **adrenaline**. It also makes the levels of **dopamine** in their blood rise. Some other chemicals in cigarettes may change how nicotine affects a person.

In some states, it's against the law to smoke in a car if there are children under a certain age there too. In Virginia, it's illegal to smoke if a child younger than eight years old is in the car.

Health Problems

Cigarettes can lead to many different health problems. Cigarettes often cause lung cancer. The chemicals in cigarettes create poisonous smoke, which contains tar that sticks to the inside of a person's lungs. Tar causes lung cancer, **emphysema**, and other lung problems.

Cigarette smoke can also cause cancer of the mouth and throat. Smoking can also cause **leukemia**, **cataracts**, and **pneumonia**. People who smoke are more likely to have heart disease or a heart attack.

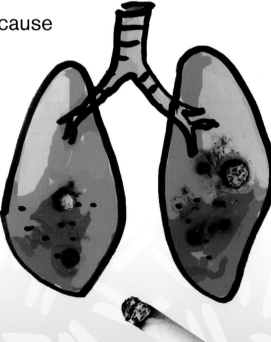

Smokers get sick more often than nonsmokers. People who smoke also have a harder time getting over colds and the flu.

Changing How You Look

Cigarettes affect a person's health, but they can also affect how a person looks. Smokers often have bigger bellies and less muscle than nonsmokers. This is because smoking pushes fat into the belly area and makes it harder for blood and **oxygen** to flow to your muscles.

Smoking can cause a person's skin to be dry and saggy, which can lead to wrinkles and other visible changes. It can also cause a person's skin to become dull and colorless. This can make a person look older than they really are.

Smoking can cause people to have yellow or brown teeth because of the nicotine and tar in tobacco. It can also cause them to have more plaque, which is a thin, sticky coating that forms on the teeth. Plaque causes gum disease, which can lead to tooth loss.

11

Affecting Others

When a person smokes, it doesn't just affect them. It also affects the people around them. Secondhand smoke is smoke from a tobacco product or the smoke a smoker has breathed out that another person breathes in. Secondhand smoke can cause many health problems in nonsmokers, such as heart disease and lung cancer.

Secondhand smoke causes even more health problems in children than adults. They may have more breathing issues, including coughing, sneezing, and shortness of breath, and may get pneumonia more often.

In the United States, many cities and states have put antismoking laws in place to keep people safe from the effects of secondhand smoke in the workplace and in public places such as restaurants.

Peer Pressure

In the United States, it's illegal for people under the age of 18 to buy tobacco products. However, that doesn't stop kids from smoking. Some kids start smoking because their parents smoke.

Other kids start smoking because of peer pressure. Peer pressure is when someone your age says something to try and force you to do something. They might say something like: "You're not cool if you don't smoke." Don't let what people say affect the things you do. Instead, just say, "No, I don't want to."

SAY NO!

People you thought were your friends might try to pressure you into smoking. Be strong and say no. It may mean that you lose a friend, but you'll be better off for it.

Why Do Adults Smoke?

Adults smoke for a number of reasons. One of the most common reasons people smoke is because they're addicted. Also, nicotine can make a person feel good. When you feel good, you might keep doing the thing that makes you feel good.

Some people also smoke because they connect smoking with doing certain activities. Smoking becomes a habit, or something that a person does often in a regular and repeated way, when they do that activity. Some people smoke because it helps them deal with their feelings.

Some people only smoke cigarettes when they're doing a certain activity. To break the pattern, the person will have to find something else to do instead of smoking.

Breaking the Habit

Smoking is a very hard habit to break. You might not like it if one of your parents or one of your brothers or sisters smokes. If you want them to quit smoking, there are some things you can do to help them.

First, tell them how you feel. If they know you don't like it when they smoke, they might be more likely to quit. Be understanding. Ask your parent, brother, or sister what you can do to help them.

If quitting is making your parent upset, you might try to do things to make them feel better. Even if they slip up and have a cigarette, be kind to them and cheer them on.

How to Quit

Quitting smoking doesn't happen overnight. It's normal for people to have setbacks when quitting. A person should first try to figure out why they want to quit. Some people might want to quit to get healthier. Other people might want to quit to save money.

Talking to a doctor is the next step. A doctor can help a person figure out how they should go about quitting. Some people quit cold turkey, which means they just stop smoking altogether. Other people quit smoking with medicine.

Nicotine patches, which are small pieces of cloth containing small amounts of nicotine, and nicotine gum can help a person quit smoking if used correctly.

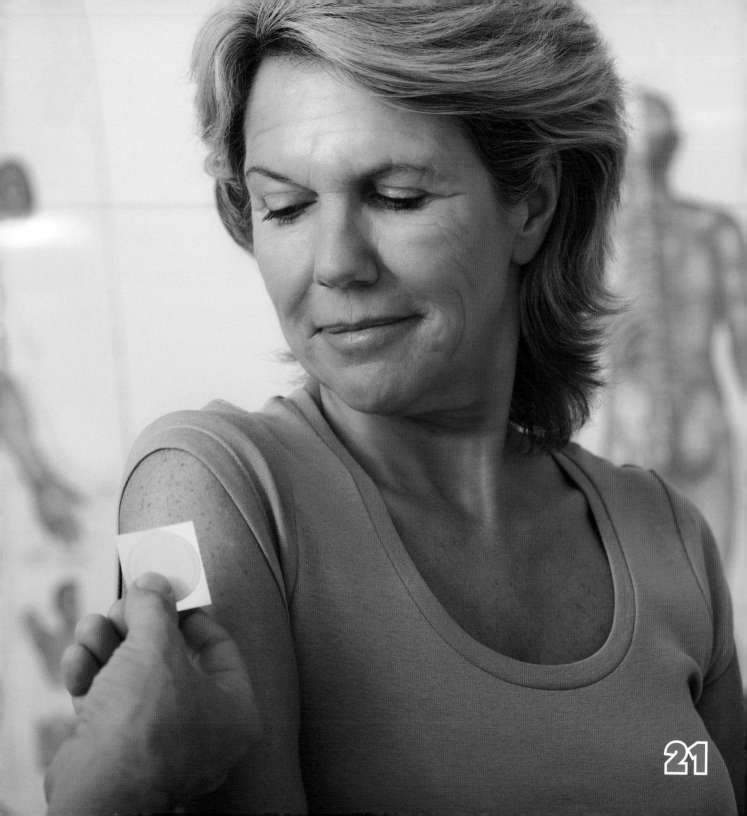

Why Is Smoking Bad?

Smoking cigarettes is bad because it's addicting and can make a person become very unhealthy. Quitting can be very hard, but it's not impossible. Going to a therapist, or a person who helps people deal with their feelings by talking about their problems, or seeing a doctor can be good first steps to quitting.

Even though smoking makes some people feel good, the bad outweighs the good. If your friends pressure you to try smoking, the best thing to say is, "No, I don't want to."

Glossary

adrenaline: A chemical that's released in the body of a person who's feeling a strong emotion. It causes the heart to beat faster and gives the person more energy.

cancer: A serious disease caused by cells that are not normal and can spread to one or many parts of the body.

cataract: A condition in which part of your eye becomes cloudy and you can't see well.

chemical: Matter that can be mixed with other matter to cause changes.

dopamine: A specific chemical that's released in the body of a person that can make them feel good.

emphysema: A disease in which the lungs become damaged and enlarged, which makes it difficult to breathe.

ingredient: One of the things that are used to make a food or a product.

leukemia: A serious disease in which too many white blood cells form.

oxygen: A chemical found in the air that has no color, taste, or smell and is necessary for life.

pneumonia: A serious disease that affects the lungs and makes it hard to breathe.

poisonous: Containing poison, a substance that can harm or kill a living thing.

Index

A

adrenaline, 6

C

cancer, 5, 6, 8, 12

cataracts, 8

chemicals, 4, 5, 6, 8

cigarettes, 4, 5, 6, 8,
        10, 16, 19, 22

D

doctor, 20, 22

dopamine, 6

E

e-cigarettes, 4, 6

emphysema, 8

H

heart, 8, 12

L

laws, 6, 13

leukemia, 8

lungs , 8, 12

N

nicotine, 6, 10, 16, 20

O

oxygen, 10

P

plaque, 10

pneumonia, 8, 12

S

secondhand smoke, 12, 13

skin, 10

T

tar, 8, 10

teeth, 10

throat, 8

tobacco, 4, 6, 10, 12, 14

U

United States, 13, 14

V

vapor, 4

Virginia, 6

Websites

Due to the changing nature of Internet links, PowerKids Press has developed an online list of websites related to the subject of this book. This site is updated regularly. Please use this link to access the list: www.powerkidslinks.com/help/smoke